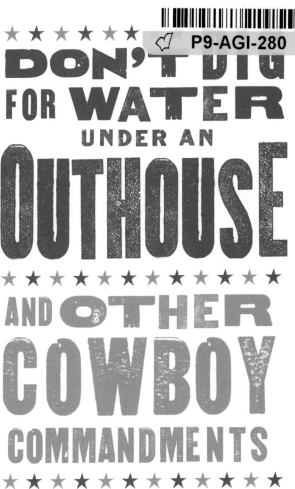

DON'T DIG
FOR WATER
UNDER AN
OUTHOUSE

AND OTHER
COWBOY
COMMANDMENTS

TEXAS BIX BENDER

GIBBS SMITH
TO ENRICH AND INSPIRE HUMANKIND
Salt Lake City | Charleston | Santa Fe | Santa Barbara

P9-AGI-280

Revised Edition
13 12   20 19 18 17 16 15 14 13 12 11 10 9 8 7 6
Text copyright © 2000 by Texas Bix Bender

All rights reserved. No part of this book may be reproduced by any means
whatsoever, either mechanical or electronic, without written permission from
the publisher, except for brief portions quoted for the purpose of review.

Published by
Gibbs Smith
P.O. Box 667
Layton, Utah 84041

Orders: 1.800.835.4993
www.gibbs-smith.com

Cover design by Black Eye Design
Printed and bound in the U.S.A.
Gibbs Smith books are printed on either recycled, 100% post-consumer
waste, FSC-certified papers or on paper produced from a 100% certified
sustainable forest/controlled wood source.

Library of Congress Cataloging-in-Publication Data

Bender, Texas Bix, 1949-
  Don't dig for water under an outhouse : and other cowboy
commandments / Texas Bix Bender. — rev. ed.
     p. cm.
  ISBN-13: 978-1-4236-0698-7
  ISBN-10: 1-4236-0698-1
  1. American wit and humor. 2. Cowboys' writings, American—West
(U.S.) 3. West (U.S.)—Social life and customs—Humor. I. Title.
  PN6165.B446 2009
  818'.5402—dc22

                    2009017195

ISBN 13: 978-0-87905-977-4 (first edition)
ISBN 10: 0-87905-977-X (first edition)

Don't let
the sun
catch you
in bed.

★ ★ ★

If it ain't right,

DON'T DO IT.

★ ★ ★

[If the boots fit,
keep getting 'em
resoled.]

★ ★ ★

What's **wanted**
isn't always
what's **needed.**

★ ★ ★

Don't let your yearnings

GET AHEAD

of your earnings.

★ ★ ★

If you value it,

take care of it.

★ ★ ★

NEVER
wear out your horse.

★ ★ ★

Spread happiness

WHERE

you go, not **when.**

★ ★ ★

If you don't feel like smiling,
give it a shot anyway.

**It'll help the general
scheme of things.**

★ ★ ★

Keep your moccasins

GREASED.

★ ★ ★

If the boot fits,
MAKE SURE
there's **two** of 'em.

★ ★ ★

For
better
or for
worse
means
FOR GOOD.

★ ★ ★

Fall in love

[*only when you can't help it.*]

* * *

Don't look
at things
for what
they're not;
look at them
for what

THEY ARE.

★ ★ ★

The side of life you see is

the side of life you show.

★ ★ ★

Never cuss
somebody else's dog
[*or abuse your own.*]

★ ★ ★

· · · · · · · · · · · · · · · ·

Control your temper
before you try to
control a horse.

· · · · · · · · · · · · · · · ·

★ ★ ★

Never take unfair advantage.

*Don't spur a horse
when he's*

SWIMMING.

★ ★ ★

NEVER MISS A GOOD CHANCE TO SHUT [UP.]

★ ★ ★

To **KNOW** *the truth,*
SPEAK *the truth.*

★ ★ ★

If it's none of your business,
stay out of it.

★ ★ ★

If it ain't
botherin' you,
leave it
ALONE.

★ ★ ★

Never take down

another man's fence.

★ ★ ★

ALWAYS

sink corner fence posts
twice as deep.

★ ★ ★

Never pick a fight with a
porcupine.

★ ★ ★

Don't forget
that there are
always
consequences.

★ ★ ★

Don't be too **SOON**
and don't be too **SELDOM.**

★ ★ ★

Never lose your
WAY HOME.

★ ★ ★

[*A lot of getting by
is gotten by
doing things you'd
rather not do.*]

★ ★ ★

When you get bucked off,
GET BACK ON.

★ ★ ★

Find the problem
before
you find the solution.

* * *

Keep only
five beans
in the wheel
and keep
the hammer
down on the

EMPTY
CHAMBER.

★ ★ ★

Try to get your wife a job
in town.

* * *

CHERISH
women,
horses,
water,
and grass.

★ ★ ★

∙ ∙ ∙ ∙ ∙ ∙ ∙ ∙ ∙ ∙

Skin
your
own
deer.

∙ ∙ ∙ ∙ ∙ ∙ ∙ ∙ ∙ ∙

★ ★ ★

Do not tolerate
weak coffee.

★ ★ ★

Never drive
black cattle
in the **DARK.**

NEVER
ride

a sore-backed horse.

★ ★ ★

If it breaks,
FIX IT.

Never **CUT** what you can **untie.**

★ ★ ★

If you can,
do it yourself,

don't ask for help.

Be a **GOOD** worker.

★ ★ ★

Never do
anything
that will
**make you afraid to
look yourself in the eye.**

★ ★ ★

Stand up **straight**
and give folks something
to look at.

★ ★ ★

If you make a mess,
CLEAN IT UP.

★ ★ ★

• • • • • • • • • • • •

A clean
saddle blanket
is more
important
than clean
sheets.

• • • • • • • • • • • •

★ ★ ★

When experience talks,
let your ears hang down and
LISTEN.

★ ★ ★

Things don't change
———————————————
as much as **YOU** do.

★ ★ ★

DEAD DUCKS
don't need killing.

★ ★ ★

The only good reason
to ride a bull
[*is to meet a nurse.*]

★ ★ ★

If you don't know
how to run it,
LEAVE IT ALONE.

★ ★ ★

Don't get
your spurs
tangled.

★ ★ ★

. . . .

Talk less and **say more.**

. . . .

★ ★ ★

Never betray a

TRUST.

★ ★ ★

When you take a
herd to water,

take 'em slow
and spread 'em out
upstream.

★ ★ ★

Never
hurry
w e a k
stock.

★ ★ ★

Keep your words
out of the
tall grass.

★ ★ ★

Don't talk down to anyone,
even if it means
gettin' off your horse.

★ ★ ★

Make **APOLOGIES,**
not **EXCUSES.**

★ ★ ★

· · · · · · · · · · · · · ·

Hold your piece
until you're sure
you know what
you're talkin' about.

· · · · · · · · · · · · · ·

★ ★ ★

Don't get even—
GET OVER IT.

★ ★ ★

{ Don't waste **good money**
on cheap boots. }

★ ★ ★

Your value
goes up and down
every day depending
on how you treat
OTHER FOLKS.

Be **kind** to animals.

★ ★ ★

Water and
truth are
freshest at their
SOURCE.

★ ★ ★

Water and soap
don't cost much;
STAY CLEAN.

★ ★ ★

If you
START IT,
stop it.

★ ★ ★

If you open it,
CLOSE IT.

★ ★ ★

It's not so much
what you call
yourself
that matters;
it's what you call
OTHERS.

★ ★ ★

Take as good a care
of your horse

as you do yourself.

★ ★ ★

Don't look for

COURAGE

in a bottle.

★ ★ ★

· · · · · · · · · · ·

Don't
go in
if you
don't know
the way
out.

· · · · · · · · · · ·

★ ★ ★

Never work for a man with
electricity in his barn.

[*You'll be up all night.*]

★ ★ ★

If you toss
your bedroll
in the wagon,
ride for the brand.

★ ★ ★

Say what you **like to hear.**

★ ★ ★

GOOD MANNERS
go a long way
towards making anybody
more attractive.

★ ★ ★

When you're heading
down a long road
with a heavy load,
don't look back,
and don't look
too far ahead,
just keep taking it
a step at a time
and you'll get there.

★ ★ ★

Help what you can;
endure what you can't.

Suspicion ain't PROOF.

★ ★ ★

Don't leave
SPUR MARKS
on a horse.

Brace your
BACKBONE

and forget your wishbone.

★ ★ ★

If you climb in the saddle,
be ready for the **RIDE.**

★　★　★

. . . .

Don't build the gate until
you've built the corral.

. . . .

★ ★ ★

Do things
when you
first know
they
NEED DOIN'.

★ ★ ★

Weigh your words,

don't count 'em.

★ ★ ★

[**NO**
whining.]

★ ★ ★

Work hard to leave
a big hole
WHEN YOU DIE.

★ ★ ★

Don't put **your** *religion in your* WIFE'S *name.*

★ ★ ★

Take your
"take home pay"
HOME.

Set the pace by the
DISTANCE.

★ ★ ★

Put off 'til tomorrow

[*what you shouldn't
be doing anyway.*]

★ ★ ★

Ride with your head, not your BUTT.

* * *

ALWAYS
cut the cards.

★ ★ ★

A full house
divided
don't win any pots.

DON'T ARGUE
just for the hell of it.

★ ★ ★

Take things by the
smooth handle.

★ ★ ★

*When somebody
does you a favor,*
remember it.

When you do a favor,
FORGET IT.

★ ★ ★

Friends last **LONGER**
the **LESS** *they are used.*

★ ★ ★

Don't do nothin' **too much.**

★ ★ ★

. . . .

A cow outfit's
never any better
than its horses.

. . . .

★ ★ ★

No poots around the
CAMPFIRE.

★ ★ ★

Never walk
BEHIND
a strange
horse.

★ ★ ★

If you say it, MEAN IT.

★ ★ ★

Don't pack hardware
for **BLUFF** or
BALLAST.

★ ★ ★

Don't worry a
GOOD THING
too hard.

★ ★ ★

[*Don't play with the cat*]
if you're the mouse.

★ ★ ★

Think twice before you put your two cents in.

Most times you won't have to spend a **penny.**

★ ★ ★

• • • • • • • • • • • •

Judge a man
by what he
DOES,
not what he
wears.

• • • • • • • • • • • •

★ ★ ★

Take pleasure
in your business.

★ ★ ★

Honor your **FATHER**
and your **MOTHER.**

★ ★ ★

Don't borrow
if you can
BUY.

★ ★ ★

DON'T DESIRE
what you can't acquire.

★ ★ ★

Do it **TODAY.**
Tomorrow is promised
to **NO ONE.**

★ ★ ★

Start **sooner,**
travel **faster,**
arrive **before you're expected.**

★ ★ ★

Keep cool,

[*but don't freeze.*]

★ ★ ★

• • • • • • • • • • • • • • • • • • •

Don't approach
bulls from the **front**
or horses from the **rear.**

• • • • • • • • • • • • • • • • • • •

★ ★ ★

THE LOSER
in a fight
ain't necessarily wrong.

★ ★ ★

Keep your
GUTS
in line
with your
gumption.

★ ★ ★

Sing, don't cry.

★ ★ ★

Never miss a chance to

DANCE.

★ ★ ★

★ Act right,
★ behave yourself,
★ do your job,
**and things will turn out
ALL RIGHT.**

★ ★ ★

Take care of your knees;

you're going to need
them all your life.

★ ★ ★

Don't wait
'til the gate's
CLOSING
to get outta
the corral.

★ ★ ★

Put away your horse

BEFORE

you put away your **dinner**.

* * *

DO YOUR BEST,

[*that's all.*]